CW01510121

KARATE VOCABULARY

A Martial Arts Handbook of 300 Essential Japanese Terms

Includes FREE MP3s of ALL the Japanese

Clay & Yumi Boutwell

Copyright © 2017-2024 Kotoba Books
www.MakotoPlus.com
www.TheJapanShop.com/bundles
www.TheJapanesePage.com

ISBN: 1547020423
ISBN-13: 978-1547020423

INTRODUCTION

Do you have a passion for martial arts? Would you like a deeper understanding of the Japanese terms and names? If so, this book is for you.

First, let me be clear: Yumi and I do not pretend to be karate experts. However, we do have a passion for the Japanese language, and many martial arts disciplines use terms, commands, and names from Japanese. This book is intended to help martial artists in that regard.

Will it help you perfect your forms or add power to your kicks? *No, not at all.* Will it help you with pronunciation and understanding of the language you hear in the dōjō? *Absolutely.*

Take "dōjō" for example. You might wonder why there are lines above the "o". That's because, in Japanese, some vowels are elongated. You may also see "dōjō" written as "doujou." So, you shouldn't say "dojo" like two quick jabs, but rather "do--jo-," lingering a bit after each vowel.

The characters (called *kanji* in Japanese) for *dōjō* look like this:

道場

Let's break that down:

道 *dō*—meaning "way" or "path" or even "teachings"

場 *jō*—meaning "place"

That's neat, right? But did you know that 道 (**dō**) is also the "dō" found in many other Japanese arts?

- 柔道 *juudō*—judo
- 書道 *shodō*—calligraphy
- 剣道 *kendō*—kendo; fencing
- 茶道 *chadō*—the tea ceremony; the way of tea
- 弓道 *kyuudō*—(Japanese) archery
- 合気道 *aikidō*—Aikido
- 武士道 *bushidō*—Bushido; way of the warrior

And many more…

道 *dō* is a very important *kanji* in the martial arts.

PRONUNCIATION

For the most part, you can pronounce the consonants as you would in English. The five vowel sounds in Japanese are like the five vowels in Spanish: a-i-u-e-o. Check the provided sound files ("aiueo.mp3") for accurate pronunciation of the vowels (see the last page for the download link).

While you do not need to know how to read any Japanese writing before using this book (rōmaji is provided), you may want to take that as your next step. If so, visit our free hiragana lesson page here: https://thejapanesepage.com/hiragana

Let's get started!

Clay & Yumi Boutwell
help@thejapanshop.com
https://www.MakotoPlus.com
http://www.TheJapanShop.com
http://www.TheJapanesePage.com

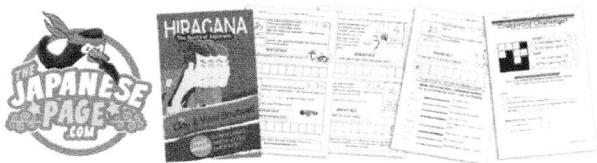
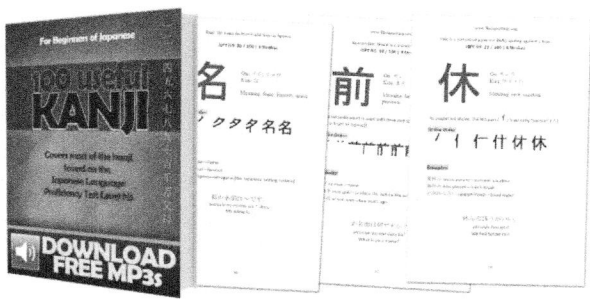

Table of Contents

Chapter One

Essential Words

空手
karate – karate

LITERALLY, "EMPTY HAND." PAY ATTENTION TO THE PRONUNCIATION. THE "TE" DOES NOT SOUND LIKE THE WORD, "TEA." [KARATE.MP3]

空
kara – empty

THIS KANJI, IN OTHER CONTEXTS, MEANS "SKY" BUT WITH *KARATE* IT MEANS EMPTY, VOID, VACANT. [KARA.MP3]

空手家
karate ka – martial artist

家 MEANS "HOUSE," BUT IN THIS CASE IT MEANS A PERFORMER OR PRACTITIONER. [KARATEKA.MP3]

武道
budō – martial way

LITERALLY, "WAY OF WARRIOR." THIS IS THE SAME KANJI (道) WE DISCUSSED IN THE INTRODUCTION. [BUDOU.MP3]

武士
bushi – warrior

ANOTHER NAME FOR "SAMURAI." [BUSHI.MP3]

武士道
bushido – **warrior's code**

THIS IS THE TRADITIONAL MORAL CODE OF THE SAMURAI, EMPHASIZING HONOR, LOYALTY, AND DISCIPLINE. [BUSHIDO.MP3]

武術
Bujutsu – **martial arts**

LITERALLY, "TECHNIQUE OF WARRIOR." [BUJUTSU.MP3]

道場

dōjō – **dojo; school; training area**

LITERALLY, "PLACE OF THE WAY." [DOUJOU.MP3]

ギ

gi – **karate uniform**

ALTHOUGH COMMON TO JUST SAY "*GI*" IN ENGLISH, IN JAPANESE, IT IS 道着 DŌGI. [GI.MP3]

帯
obi – **belt**

THE OBI IS ALSO THE LARGE "BELT" AROUND A KIMONO. [OBI.MP3]

はい

hai – **yes**

THE MOST COMMON WAY TO SAY "YES." HAI.MP3

いいえ

iie – **no**

PRONOUNCE THE *II* LONG OTHERWISE YOU WILL BE SAYING "*IE*" WHICH MEANS "HOUSE." IIE.MP3

先生

sensei – **teacher**

LITERALLY, "ALIVE BEFORE." (SOMEONE WHO COMES BEFORE) IT IS USED TO REFER TO TEACHERS, DOCTORS, PASTORS, AND OTHER PEOPLE OF AUTHORITY. [SENSEI.MP3]

先輩

sempai – **someone senior to oneself**

WE USED A ROMANIZED "M" BECAUSE THAT IS THE CLOSER SOUND IN THIS CASE, BUT JAPANESE ん IS USUALLY PRONOUNCED AS "N." [SEMPAI.MP3]

形

kata – **kata; form**

ALSO WRITTEN WITH THIS KANJI, 型. [KATA.MP3]

刀

katana – **(long) sword**

[KATANA.MP3]

剣術

kenjutsu – **art of the sword; fencing**

LITERALLY, THE ART/TECHNIQUE OF THE BLADE. A HISTORICAL MARTIAL ART
PRIMARILY FOR SAMURAI, DISTINCT FROM MODERN 剣道 (KENDŌ)
[KENJUTSU.MP3]

気

ki – **energy; spirit**

KI IS ONE OF THOSE KANJI THAT HAS A MULTITUDE OF MEANINGS AND
USAGES. IT CAN MEAN MIND, SPIRIT, INTENT, MOOD, FEELING,
ATMOSPHERE, AND IS FOUND IN A HOST OF IDIOMATIC EXPRESSIONS.
[KI.MP3]

元気

genki — healthy; spirited

TO ASK, "HOW ARE YOU?" SAY, "*OGENKI DESU KA?*" [GENKI.MP3]

技

waza — technique; skill; craft

THIS CAN ALSO BE PRONOUNCED, "*GI.*" [WAZA.MP3]

段

dan — degree; grade

USED TO DENOTE RANKS IN MARTIAL ARTS, WITH "DAN" BEING ADVANCED AND "KYUU" BEING INTRODUCTORY/INTERMEDIATE [DAN.MP3]

級

kyuu — class; rank

一級 *IKKYUU*—FIRST CLASS/TOP LEVEL [KYUU.MP3]

息吹

ibuki — breathing techniques

息 BREATH ＋ 吹 BLOW OUT [IBUKI.MP3]

術

jutsu – art (of combat)

THIS CAN MEAN ART, TECHNIQUE, SKILL, TRICK, AND EVEN MAGIC.
EXAMPLES INCLUDE 忍術 (NINJUTSU, ART OF STEALTH) OR 柔術 (JŪJUTSU,
ART OF PLIABILITY) [JUTSU.MP3]

Chapter Two

General Karate Vocabulary

下

shita — **down**

THE SMALLER HORIZONTAL LINE TILTS DOWNWARD BELOW THE LARGER LINE, SYMBOLIZING 'DOWN.' [SHITA.MP3]

上

ue — **up; above**

THE SMALLER HORIZONTAL LINE IS ABOVE THE LARGER ONE, REPRESENTING 'UP.' [UE.MP3]

左

hidari — **left**

"*HIDARI ASHI*" LEFT FOOT; "*HIDARI TE*" LEFT HAND; COMMON IN DIRECTIONAL COMMANDS SUCH AS 'HIDARI GAMAE' (LEFT STANCE). [HIDARI.MP3]

右

migi — **right**

"MIGI ASHI" RIGHT FOOT; "*MIGI TE*" RIGHT HAND; OFTEN USED IN COMMANDS LIKE 'MIGI GAMAE' (RIGHT STANCE). [MIGI.MP3]

前

Mae — front

"*DŌJŌ NO MAE*" IN FRONT OF THE DOJO; USED TO DESCRIBE FACING FORWARD OR POSITIONING AT THE FRONT, SUCH AS 'MAE GERI' (FRONT KICK). [MAE.MP3]

うしろ

ushiro — back; behind

"*DŌJŌ NO USHIRO*" BEHIND THE DOJO; USED IN MOVES LIKE 'USHIRO GERI' (BACK KICK). [USHIRO.MP3]

横

yoko — side

"*HITO NO YOKO*" THE SIDE OF A PERSON; COMMON IN TECHNIQUES LIKE 'YOKO GERI' (SIDE KICK). [YOKO.MP3]

回し

mawashi — around

THIS CAN REFER TO CIRCULAR MOVEMENTS ('MAWASHI GERI' OR ROUNDHOUSE KICK) OR ALSO THE SUMO WRESTLER'S BELT. [MAWASHI.MP3]

右回り

migi mawari – **rotating right**

DESCRIBES A CLOCKWISE MOTION, OFTEN USED IN KATA MOVEMENTS OR PARTNER DRILLS. [MIGIMAWARI.MP3]

左回り

hidari mawari – **rotating left**

REFERS TO A COUNTERCLOCKWISE MOTION. [HIDARIMAWARI.MP3]

上段

jōdan – **upper area**

THIS REFERS TO STRIKES OR BLOCKS TARGETING THE HEAD AND THROAT AREA, SUCH AS 'JŌDAN UKE' (UPPER BLOCK). HEAD AND THROAT [JOUDAN.MP3]

中段

chuudan – **middle area**

TARGETS THE TORSO, TYPICALLY BETWEEN THE BELT AND COLLAR, AS IN 'CHŪDAN TSUKI' (MIDDLE PUNCH). [CHUUDAN.MP3]

下段

gedan – **lower area**

REFERS TO THE AREA BELOW THE BELT, COMMONLY SEEN IN 'GEDAN BARAI' (DOWNWARD BLOCK). [GEDAN.MP3]

気合い

kiai – scream; yell; fighting spirit

THIS IS A SHORT, SHARP SHOUT USED TO FOCUS ENERGY, INTIMIDATE AN OPPONENT, OR TIME STRIKES. KIAI IS AN ESSENTIAL ASPECT OF KARATE. LITERALLY, "UNION OF ENERGY." [KIAI.MP3]

呼吸

kokyuu – breath; respiration

呼 CALL OUT TO + 吸 INHALE [KOKYUU.MP3]

棒

bō – stick; pole

AS A WEAPON [BOU.MP3]

棒術

bō jutsu – art of fighting with a *bō* (pole)

OFTEN, AS IN THIS RECORDING, "JUTSU" IS PRONOUNCED MORE LIKE "JITSU." [BOUJUTSU.MP3]

巻き藁

maki wara – **punching board; straw post for sword strikes, punches, and arrow hits**

巻き MAKI (ROLLED UP) + 藁 WARA (STRAW) [MAKIWARA.MP3]

黙想

mokusō – **meditation**

黙 MOKU (SILENCE) + 想 SŌ (THOUGHT) [MOKUSOU.MP3]

分解

bunkai – **examining katas**

LITERALLY, "ANALYSIS." [BUNKAI.MP3]

逆

gyaku – **reverse; opposite**

[GYAKU.MP3]

万歳

banzai – **banzai!**

LITERALLY, "10,000 YEARS OLD." USUALLY, THIS IS SAID THREE TIMES WHILE RAISING ONE'S HANDS [BANZAI.MP3]

Chapter Three

Kata

太極初段
Taikyoku shodan

太極 *TAIKYOKU* IN CHINESE PHILOSOPHY MEANS THE FIRST THINGS (PRINCIPLE THAT EMBODIES ALL POTENTIAL, TIME AND SPACE). 初段 *SHODAN* MEANS "FIRST (LOWEST) GRADE" [TAIKYOKUSHODAN.MP3]

平安初段
Heian shodan

平安 *HEIAN* MEANS "PEACE" OR "TRANQUILITY" AND IS BEST KNOWN AS THE NAME OF THE ANCIENT HEIAN ERA (794-1185) [HEIANSHODAN.MP3]

平安二段
Heian nidan

二段 NIDAN SIMPLY MEANS "SECOND STEP/GRADE" [HEIANNIDAN.MP3]

平安三段
Heian sandan

三段 SANDAN MEANS "THIRD STEP/GRADE" [HEIANSANDAN.MP3]

平安四段
Heian yondan

THIS MAY BE PRONOUNCED "*YODAN*" (WITHOUT THE FIRST "N") ALSO, BUT "*YONDAN*" APPEARS TO BE MORE COMMON. [HEIANYONDAN.MP3]

平安五段
Heian godan

五段 *GODAN* MEANS "FIFTH STEP/GRADE." [HEIANGODAN.MP3]

披塞大
Bassai dai

OR *PASSAI DAI* [BASSAIDAI.MP3]

披塞小
Bassai shō

LITERALLY, "SMALL EXPOSED BLOCK." [BASSAISHOU.MP3]

慈恩
Jion

慈 JI (MERCY) + 恩 ON (GRACE; KINDNESS) [JION.MP3]

燕飛
Enpi

EN (SWALLOW (BIRD)) + *PI* (TO FLY) [ENPI.MP3]

観空大
Kanku dai

KAN (VIEW) + KU (SKY) + DAI (LARGE) [KANKUDAI.MP3]

観空小
Kankū shō

KAN (OUTLOOK) + KUU (EMPTY/AIR) + SHOU (SMALL) [KANKUUSHOU.MP3]

半月
Hangetsu

LITERALLY, HALF-MOON. [HANGETSU.MP3]

十手
Jitte

A SHORT TRUNCHEON WITH A HOOK [JITTE.MP3]

岩鶴
Gankaku

GAN (BOULDER; ROCK) + *KAKU* (CRANE (BIRD)) [GANKAKU.MP3]

鉄騎初段
Tekki shodan

[TEKKISHODAN.MP3]

鉄騎二段
Tekki nidan

TEK- (IRON) + *KI* (HORSE RIDING) [TEKKINIDAN.MP3]

鉄騎三段
Tekki sandan

[TEKKISANDAN.MP3]

二十四歩
Nijūshiho

LITERALLY, 24 STEPS. [NIJUUSHIHO.MP3]

珍手
Chinte

CHIN (RARE) + *TE* (HAND) [CHINTE.MP3]

壯鎭
Sōchin

SŌ (ROBUST; LARGE) + *CHIN* (ANCIENT PEACE-PRESERVATION CENTER) [SOUCHIN.MP3]

明鏡
Meikyō

LITERALLY, "CLEAR MIRROR." [MEIKYOU.MP3]

雲手
Unsu

UN (CLOUD) + *SU* (HAND) [UNSU.MP3]

王冠
Wankan

LITERALLY, "CROWN." [WANKAN.MP3]

五十四歩小
Gojūshiho shō

LITERALLY, "54 STEPS SMALL." [GOJUUSHIHOSHOU.MP3]

五十四歩大
Gojūshiho dai

LITERALLY, "54 STEPS LARGE." [GOJUUSHIHODAI.MP3]

慈陰
Ji'in

JI (MERCY) + *IN* (SECRET; SHADOW) [JIIN.MP3]

And here are the 剛柔流 Goujuu-Ryuu kata in Japanese:
(See the "Goujuu-Ryuu" folder for sound)

Kihon (基本): The Basics

- 三戦 (Sanchin) - Three Battles

Kaishu Kata (開手形): Open Hand Form

- 撃砕大一 (Gekisai Dai Ichi) - Attack and Smash 1

- 撃砕大二 (Gekisai Dai Ni) - Attack and Smash 2

- 砕破 (Saifa) - Tear and Smash

- 制引戦 (Seiyunchin) - Control and Pull in Battle

- 四向戦 (Shisochin) - Battle of Four Directions

- 三十六手 (Sanseiru) - 36 Hands

- 十八手 (Sepai) - 18 Hands

- 久留頓破 (Kururunfa) - Holding Ground

- 十三手 (Seisan) - 13 Hands

- 壱百零八手 (Suparinpei) - 108 Hands

Heishu Kata (閉手形): Closed Hand Form

- 転掌 (Tensho) - Rotating Palms

Chapter Four

Dojo Kun (Training hall rules) for Shōtōkan Karate

These rules (or variations on them) are often posted at the entrance to the *dōjō*.

一、人格完成に努むること

hitotsu, jinkaku kansei ni tsutomuru koto

Each person must strive for the perfection of one's character.

JINKAKU (PERSON'S CHARACTER); *KANSEI NI* (TO PERFECT); *TSUTOMURU* (TO STRIVE) [DOJOKUN1.MP3]

一、誠の道を守ること

hitotsu, makoto no michi o mamoru koto

Each person must protect the way of truth.

MAKOTO NO MICHI (THE WAY OF TRUTH); MAMORU (PROTECT) [DOJOKUN2.MP3]

一、努力の精神を養うこと

hitotsu, doryōku no seishin o yashinau koto

Each person must endeavour (fostering the spirit of effort).

DŌRYOKU (EFFORT); *SEISHIN* (SPIRIT); *YASHINAU* (CULTIVATE) [DOJOKUN3.MP3]

一、礼儀を重んずること

hitotsu, reigi o omonzuru koto

Each person must respect others and the rules of etiquette.

REIGI (COURTESY); *OMONZURU* (HONOR); [DOJOKUN4.MP3]

30

一、血気の勇を戒むること

hitotsu, kekki no yū o imashimuru koto

Each person must refrain from violent behavior (guard against impetuous courage).

KEKKI (IMPETUOUS VIGOR); *YUU* (COURAGE); *IMASHIMURU* (REFRAIN)

[DOJOKUN5.MP3]

Chapter Five

Niju Kun, the Twenty Instructions of Shōtōkan Karate

しょうとうかん
松濤館

[SHOTOKAN.MP3]

These twenty instructions were developed by the Okinawan martial arts master Gichin Funakoshi.

The instructions are not numbered, but often begin with the word, 一つ *hitotsu*, meaning "One…"

The name means "pine – wave – palace."

空手道は礼に始まり礼に終る事を忘るな。

karate-do wa rei ni hajimari rei ni owaru koto o wasaru na.

Do not forget: Karate begins and ends with *rei* (bow).

HAJIMARI (BEGIN); *OWARU* (END); *WASURU NA* (DON'T FORGET)
[NIJUKUN1.MP3]

空手に先手なし。

karate ni sente nashi.

There is no first strike in karate.

SENTE (FIRST STRIKE); NASHI (IS NOT) [NIJUKUN2.MP3]

空手は義の補け。

karate wa, gi no tasuke.

Karate stands on the side of justice.

GI (RIGHTEOUSNESS); *TASUKE* (HELPER) [NIJUKUN3.MP3]

先づ自己を知れ而して他を知れ。

mazu onore o shire, shikashite ta o shire.

First know yourself, then know others.

ONORE (ONESELF); *SHIRE* (TO KNOW); *SHIKASHITE* (AND THEN); *TA* (OTHERS)
[NIJUKUN4.MP3]

技術より心術。

gijitsu yori shinjitsu.

Mentality over technique.

GIJITSU (SKILL TECHNIQUE); *YORI* (LESS THAN); *SHINJITSU* (HEART TECHNIQUE) [NIJUKUN5.MP3]

心は放たん事を要す。

kokoro wa hanatan koto o yosu.

The mind must be set free.

KOKORO (HEART); *HANATA* (RELEASED); *YOSU* (NEED; MAIN POINT) [NIJUKUN6.MP3]

禍は懈怠に生ず 。

wazawai wa ketai ni seizu.

Calamity springs from carelessness.

WAZAWAI (CALAMITY); *KETAI* (LAZY NEGLECT); *SEI* (BIRTHED) [NIJUKUN7.MP3]

道場のみの空手と思うな。

dojo nomi no karate to omō na.

Karate goes beyond the dojo. [Literally, Don't think karate is only for the dojo.]

NOMI (ONLY); *OMOU NA* (DON'T THINK) [NIJUKUN8.MP3]

空手の修業は一生である。

karate-do no shugyo wa issho de aru.

Karate is a lifelong pursuit.

SHUGYO (TRAINING); ISSHO (LIFELONG) [NIJUKUN9.MP3]

凡ゆるものを空手化せよ其処に妙味あり。

ara yuru mono o karateka seyo; sokoni myomi ari.

Apply the way of karate to all things. Therein lies its beauty.

ARA YURU (ALL; EVERY); MONO (THING); KA (APPLY; INFLUENCE); SOKONI (IN THAT); MYOMI (EXQUISITE CHARM; PROFIT) [NIJUKUN10.MP3]

空手は湯の如し、絶えず熱度を与えざれば元の水に還る。

karate wa yu no gotoshi, taezu netsu o atae zareba motono mizu ni kaeru.

Karate is like boiling water; without heat, it returns to its tepid state.

YU (BOILING WATER); GOTOSHI (LIKE; COMPARED TO); TAEZU (CONSTANTLY); NETSU (HEAT); ATAEZAREBA (IF NOT GIVEN); MIZU NI (INTO (COLD) WATER); KAERU (RETURN) [NIJUKUN11.MP3]

勝つ考は持つな、負けぬ考は必要。

katsu kangae wa motsuna; makenu kangae wa hitsuyo.

Do not think of winning. Think, rather, of not losing.

KATSU (WIN); KANGAE (THINKING); MOTSUNA (DON'T HOLD (THOUGHT));
MAKENU (DON'T LOSE); HITSUYO (NECESSARY) [NIJUKUN12.MP3]

敵に因って轉化せよ。

tekki ni yotte tenka seyo.

Make adjustments according to your opponent

TEKI (ENEMY); YOTTE (ACCORDING TO); TENKA (ADJUST) [NIJUKUN13.MP3]

戦は虚実の操縦如何に在り。

tatakai wa kyojitsu no soju ikan ni ari.

**The outcome of a battle depends on how one handles emptiness
and fullness (weakness and strength).**

TATAKAI (BATTLE); KYOJITSU (TRUTH OR FALSEHOOD); SOJU IKAN (HOW ONE
MANAGES) [NIJUKUN14.MP3]

人の手足を劍と思へ。

hito no te ashi wa ken to omoe.

Think of hands and feet as swords.

HITO (PERSON); TEASHI (HANDS AND FEET); KEN (SWORD); OMOE (THINK)
[NIJUKUN15.MP3]

男子門を出づれば百万の敵あり。

danshi mon o izureba hyakuman no teki ari.

When you step beyond your own gate, you face a million enemies.

DANSHI (YOUNG MAN); *MON* (GATE); *IZUREBA* (LEAVE); *HYAKUMAN* (1,000,000); *TEKI* (ENEMIES) [NIJUKUN16.MP3]

構は初心者に後は自然体。

kamae wa shoshinsha ni atowa shizentai.

Kamae is for beginners; later, one stands in shizentai.

KAMAE (POSTURE); *SHOSHINSHA* (BEGINNER); *ATO* (AFTER) *SHIZENTAI* (NATURAL STATE/STANCE) [NIJUKUN17.MP3]

形は正しく実戦は別物。

kata wa tadashiku, jisen wa betsumono.

Perform kata exactly; actual combat is another matter.

KATA (KATA; FORM); *TADASHIKU* (CORRECTLY); *JISEN* (ACTUAL BATTLE); *BETSUMONO* (DIFFERENT MATTER) [NIJUKUN18.MP3]

力の強弱体の伸縮技の緩急を忘るな。

chikara no kyojaku tai no shinshuku waza no kankyu o wasuruna.

Do not forget the employment of withdrawal of power, the

extension or contraction of the body, the swift or leisurely application of technique.

CHIKARA (POWER); *KYOJAKU TAI* (STRENGTH OF BODY); *SHINSHUKU* (FLEXIBILITY); *KANKYU* (SLOW AND FAST); *WASURUNA* (DON'T FORGET) [NIJUKUN19.MP3]

常に思念工夫せよ。
tsune ni shinen ku fu seyo.
Be constantly mindful and resourceful.

TSUNE NI (ALWAYS); *SHINEN* (THOUGHT); *KUFU* (SCHEME; DEVISING) [NIJUKUN20.MP3]

Chapter Six

Kicks

蹴り
keri − kick

WHEN FOLLOWING OTHER WORDS, THE "K" CHANGES TO A "G" SOUND AS IN *MAE GERI* (FRONT KICK). ALTHOUGH COMMON, IT SHOULD NOT BE PRONOUNCED "*GERI*" BY ITSELF--THIS COULD MEAN "DIARRHEA."
[KERI.MP3]

後ろ蹴り
ushiro geri − back kick

"*USHIRO*" BACK + "*KERI*" KICK--THE "K" CHANGES TO THE HARDER "G."
[USHIROGERI.MP3]

前蹴り
mae geri − front kick

MAE (FRONT) + *GERI* (KICK) [MAEGERI.MP3]

回し蹴り
mawashi geri − roundhouse kick

MAWASHI MEANS "REVOLVE" [MAWASHIGERI.MP3]

横蹴り

yoko geri – **side kick**

YOKO (SIDE) [YOKOGERI.MP3]

金蹴り

kin geri – **groin kick**

KIN MEANS GOLD, BUT IN COLLOQUIAL JAPANESE, IT CAN MEAN TESTICLES.
[KINGERI.MP3]

踵蹴り

kakato geri – **heel kick**

KAKATO (HEEL (OF FOOT)) [KAKATOGERI.MP3]

三日月蹴り

mikazuki geri – **crescent kick**

MIKAZUKI MEANS "NEW MOON" OR "CRESCENT MOON."
[MIKAZUKIGERI.MP3]

膝蹴り

hiza geri – **knee kick**

HIZA (KNEE) [HIZAGERI.MP3]

跳び蹴り

tobi geri − **jump kick**

TOBI MEANS "JUMP." [TOBIGERI.MP3]

Chapter Seven

Stances

用意立ち

yōi dachi — ready stance

YOI (PREPARATION) + *TACHI* (STANDING) [YOUIDACHI.MP3]

後屈立ち

kōkutsu dachi — back leaning stance

KŌKUTSU (TURN BACK) [KOUKUTSUDACHI.MP3]

前屈立ち

zenkutsu dachi — forward leaning stance

LITERALLY, "BEND FORWARD STANCE." [ZANKUTSUDACHI.MP3]

逆前屈立ち

gyaku zenkutsu dachi — reverse forward leaning stance

GYAKU (REVERSE); *ZENKUTSU* (BEND FORWARD); *DACHI* (STANDING)
[GYAKUZENKUTSUDACHI.MP3]

三戦立ち

sanchin dachi — hour glass stance / three-point stance

LITERALLY, "THREE BATTLE STANCE." [SANCHINDACHI.MP3]

組手立ち

kumite dachi – **sparring stance**

KUMITE (PAIRED KARATE KATA) [KUMITEDACHI.MP3]

猫足立ち

neko ashi dachi – **cat stance**

NEKO (CAT); ASHI (FOOT); DACHI (STANCE) [NEKOASHIDACHI.MP3]

騎馬立ち

kiba dachi – **horse riding stance**

KIBA (HORSE RIDING) [KIBADACHI.MP3]

後屈立ち

kōkutsu dachi – **back stance**

LITERALLY, "BACK BENDING STANCE." [KOUKUTSUDACHI.MP3]

四股立ち

shiko dachi – **straddle/squat stance**

THE 四股 SHIKO IS THE CEREMONIAL LEG RAISING AND STOMPING BY SUMO WRESTLERS. [SHIKODACHI.MP3]

八字立ち

hachiji dachi – **natural stance; figure eight stance**

LITERALLY, "FIGURE EIGHT STANCE." [HACHIJIDACHI.MP3]

結び立ち

musubi dachi – **attention stance**

LITERALLY, "CONCLUDED STANCE." [MUSUBIDACHI.MP3]

Chapter Eight

Blocks

受け

uke – **block**

LITERALLY, "RECEIVE." [UKE.MP3]

上受け

uwa uke – **rising block**

BLOCKING THE UPPER AREA (JŌDAN) [UWAUKE.MP3]

内受け

uchi uke – **inside block**

BLOCKING THE MID AREA (CHUUDAN) [UCHIUKE.MP3]

横受け

yoko uke – **side block**

BLOCKING THE MID AREA (CHUUDAN) [YOKOUKE.MP3]

下段払い

gedan barai – **lower sweep; lower block**

PARRYING THE LOWER AREA (GEDAN) [GEDANBARAI.MP3]

外受け

soto uke – **outside block**

LITERALLY, "OUTSIDE RECEIVE." [SOTOUKE.MP3]

回し受け

mawashi uke – **roundhouse (circular) block**

"*MAWASHI*" MEANS "GOING AROUND." [MAWASHIUKE.MP3]

手刀受け

shutō uke – **knife hand block**

SHUTŌ (HAND USED LIKE A SWORD IN STRIKING) [SHUTOUUKE.MP3]

裏拳受け

uraken uke – **back fist block**

URAKEN (BACK FIST) [URAKENUKE.MP3]

背手受け

haishu uke – **back hand block**

LITERALLY THE BACK (背) AND HAND (手) [HAISHUUKE.MP3]

上段受け

jōdan uke – **upper level block**

[JOUDANUKE.MP3]

中段受け

chuudan uke – **middle level block**

[CHUUDANUKE.MP3]

手外受け

te soto uke – **knife hand block**

[TESOTOUKE.MP3]

十字受け

juuji uke – **cross block**

JUUJI (CROSS) [JUUJIUKE.MP3]

かげ受け

kage uke – **shadow block**

KAGE (SHADOW) [KAGEUKE.MP3]

上げ受け

age uke – **rising block**

AGE (RISE; ELEVATE) [AGEUKE.MP3]

Chapter Nine

Punches

突き

tsuki – **punch; strike**

WHEN COMBINED WITH OTHER WORDS, THE "*TSU*" BECOMES "*ZU*" AS BELOW. [TSUKI.MP3]

裏拳突き

uraken zuki – **back fist strike**

URA (BACK) + KEN (FIST) [URAKENZUKI.MP3]

手刀

shutō – **knife hand**

LITERALLY "HAND SWORD." DESCRIBES USING ONE'S HAND AS A SWORD. [SHUTOU.MP3]

手刀打ち

shutō uchi – **knife hand strike**

SHU (HAND) TOU (SWORD) [SHUTOUUCHI.MP3]

上段突き

jōdan zuki – **high punch**

JŌDAN (UPPER AREA) [JOUDANZUKI.MP3]

中段突き

chuudan zuki – **middle punch**

CHUUDAN (MIDDLE AREA) [CHUUDANZUKI.MP3]

縦突き

tate zuki – **tatezuki; vertical punch**

TATE (VERTICAL) [TATEZUKI.MP3]

二段突き

nidan zuki – **double punch**

NIDAN (SECOND STEP) [NIDANZUKI.MP3]

貫手

nukite – **spear hand**

NUKI (PIERCE) [NUKITE.MP3]

下突き

shita zuki – **upper cut**

LITERALLY, "(FROM) BELOW STRIKE." [SHITAZUKI.MP3]

四本貫手

yonhon nukite – **four fingered spear hand**

FINGERS ARE COUNTED IN JAPANESE USING "*HON*": *YON* (4) + *HON* = FOUR
FINGERS [YONHONNUKITE.MP3]

二本貫手

nihon nukite – **two fingered spear hand**

FINGERS ARE COUNTED IN JAPANESE USING "*HON*": *NI* (2) + *HON* = TWO
FINGERS [NIHONNUKITE.MP3]

一本貫手

ippon nukite – **single finger spear hand**

FINGERS ARE COUNTED IN JAPANESE USING "*HON*," BUT IN THIS CASE TWO
THINGS CHANGE: *ICHI* (1) TRUNCATES AND THE "H" CHANGES TO THE
HARDER "P." [IPPONNUKITE.MP3]

背手打ち

haishu uchi – **back hand strike**

LITERALLY THE BACK (背) AND HAND (手) [HAISHUUCHI.MP3]

逆突き

gyaku tsuki – **reverse punch**

GYAKU (REVERSE) [GYAKUTSUKI.MP3]

追突き

oi tsuki – **lunge punch**

OI (TO CHASE) [OITSUKI.MP3]

裏拳

uraken – **backfist**

URA (THE BACK) [URAKEN.MP3]

背刀

haitō – **ridge hand**

HAI (BACK) + TŌ (BLADE) [HAITOU.MP3]

手槌

tetsui – **hammer fist**

LITERALLY, HAND HAMMER. [TETSUI.MP3]

上げ突き

agetsuki – **upper cut**

[AGETSUKI.MP3]

掌底

shōtei – **palm heel**

SHŌ (PALM OF HAND) + *TEI* (BOTTOM) [SHOUTEI.MP3]

手刀

tegatana – **hand sword**

LITERALLY, "HAND SWORD." [TEGATANA.MP3]

回し突き

mawashi tsuki – **round house punch**

MAWASHI (REVOLVE; GO AROUND) [MAWASHITSUKI.MP3]

試し割り

tameshi wari – **breaking (wood; stone; etc)**

"*TAMESHI*" MEANS "TO TRY" AND "*WARI*" MEANS "TO BREAK."
[TAMESHIWARI.MP3]

Chapter Ten

Sparring and Other

投げ

nage – **throw**

FROM THE VERB 投げる *NAGERU* TO THROW. [NAGE.MP3]

投げ技

nage waza – **throwing techniques**

WAZA (TECHNIQUE) [NAGEWAZA.MP3]

組手

kumite – **sparring**

LITERALLY, GROUP (OF) HANDS. [KUMITE.MP3]

一本組手

ippon kumite – **one step sparring**

[IPPONKUMITE.MP3]

三本組手

san bon kumite – **three step sparring**

[SANBONKUMITE.MP3]

自由組手

jiyuu kumite – free style sparring

"*JIYUU*" MEANS "FREE" AS IN FREEDOM. [JIYUUKUMITE.MP3]

組手試合

kumite shiai – sparring match

A "*SHIAI*" IS A COMPETITIVE CONTEST OR TOURNAMENT FOR ANY SPORT. [KUMITESHIAI.MP3]

すり足

suri ashi – shuffle; gliding movement

THIS IS ALSO A SUMO EXERCISE OF MOVING ONE'S FEET WITHOUT LIFTING OFF THE GROUND. [SURIASHI.MP3]

前受け身

mae ukemi – forward breakfall

MAE (FRONT) [MAEUKEMI.MP3]

横受け身

yoko ukemi – sideways breakfall

YOKO (SIDE) [YOKOUKEMI.MP3]

後ろ受け身

ushiro ukemi – **backwards breakfall**

USHIRO (BACK; BEHIND) [USHIROUKEMI.MP3]

回転受け身

kaiten ukemi – **rolling breakfall**

KAITEN (ROTATION; REVOLVING) [KAITENUKEMI.MP3]

足の甲

ashi no kō – **instep**

LITERALLY, FOOT SHELL. [ASHINOKOU.MP3]

当て身技

atemi waza – **attack to vitals**

ATEMI (STRIKE; BLOW) [ATEMIWAZA.MP3]

Chapter Eleven

Commands

はじめ

hajime – **begin**

FROM *HAJIMERU* (TO BEGIN) [HAJIME.MP3]

気をつけ

ki o tsuke – **attention**

LITERALLY, APPLY YOUR *KI* (SPIRIT; MIND; THOUGHTS). [KIOTSUKE.MP3]

止め

yame – **stop**

[YAME.MP3]

待て

mate – **stop (wait)**

FROM *MATSU* (TO WAIT). [MATE.MP3]

礼

rei – **bow; express thanks**

BE SURE TO KEEP YOUR BACK AS STRAIGHT AS POSSIBLE. [REI.MP3]

回って

mawatte – turn around (command)

THE -*TE* MAKES THIS A COMMAND; TO BE MORE POLITE, ADD "*KUDASAI.*" [MAWATTE.MP3]

立って

tatte – stand up (command)

FROM *TATSU* (TO STAND). [TATTE.MP3]

起立

kiritsu – command to stand up at attention

THIS IS ALSO SAID IN SCHOOLS. AS THE TEACHER ENTERS THE ROOM, THE STUDENTS SAY THIS AND STAND. [KIRITSU.MP3]

座って

suwatte – sit down (command)

FROM *SUWARU* (TO SIT). [SUWATTE.MP3]

休め

yasume – relax; at ease

FROM *YASUMERU* (TO REST; TO GIVE RELIEF) [YASUME.MP3]

よい

yoi – **prepare**

[YOI.MP3]

足をかえて

ashi o kaete – **change leg (stance)**

ASHI (LEG); *KAETE* (CHANGE) [ASHIOKAETE.MP3]

手をかえて

te o kaete – **change hand (position)**

TE (HAND); *KAETE* (CHANGE) [TEOKAETE.MP3]

斉列

seiretsu – **line up (command)**

SEI (EQUAL; SIMILAR); *RETSU* (FILE; ROW; LINE) [SEIRETSU.MP3]

足交代

ashi kōtai – **alternate feet**

THIS CAN BE A COMMAND TO SWITCH FEET. [ASHIKOUTAI.MP3]

着座

chaku za – kneeling into *seiza* sitting position

THIS CAN BE A COMMAND TO SIT IN SEIZA POSITION. SEIZA IS A TRADITIONAL WAY OF SITTING WITH ONE'S LEGS UNDER ONE'S BUTTOCKS. [CHAKUZA.MP3]

構えて

kamaete – get into position (command)

[KAMAETE.MP3]

戻って

modotte – return to position (command)

FROM *MODORU* (TO RETURN; COME BACK) [MODOTTE.MP3]

もう一度

mō ichido – one more time

MOU (ALSO; FURTHER; AGAIN); *ICHI DO* (ONE TIME) [MOUICHIDO.MP3]

並んで

narande – line up (command)

FROM *NARABU* (TO LINE UP) [NARANDE.MP3]

押忍

osu – **karate greeting**

ALSO "OSSU." IT IS ALSO A GREETING BETWEEN CLOSE MALES. [OSU.MP3]

Chapter Twelve

Numbers

NINJA PENGUIN MINI LESSON

Counting People

Japanese is filled with counters. English has a few (a cup of coffee). The counter for people is 人 nin. But! the first two are irregular.

一人 *hitori* one person [irregular]

二人 *futari* two people [irregular]

三人 *sannin* three people

四人 *yonin* four people [note "yonin" not "yonnin"]

五人 *gonin* five people

六人 *rokunin* six people

七人 *shichinin / nananin* seven people [two pronunciations]

八人 *hachinin* eight people

九人 *kyuunin / kunin* nine people [two pronunciations]

十人 *juunin* ten people

After two, just add "*nin*" to the number.

一

ichi – **one**

JAPANESE USES TWO SETS OF NUMBERS FOR 1-10--SOUNDS BORROWED FROM CHINESE AND NATIVE JAPANESE SOUNDS. NUMBERS ABOVE 10 USE THE CHINESE SOUNDS. YOU MAY WANT TO LEARN THE CHINESE SOUNDS FIRST AS THEY ARE MORE USEFUL (PRESENTED HERE). [ICHI.MP3]

二

ni – **two**

[NI.MP3]

三

san – **three**

[SAN.MP3]

四

shi – **four**

NOTE: BOTH "*SHI*" AND "*YON*" ARE USED FOR 4. LEARN BOTH AND NOTE THE CONTEXT WHERE EACH IS USED. [SHI.MP3]

四

yon – **four**

NOTE: BOTH "*SHI*" AND "*YON*" ARE USED FOR 4. LEARN BOTH AND NOTE THE CONTEXT WHERE EACH IS USED. [YON.MP3]

五

go – **five**

[GO.MP3]

六

roku – **six**

[ROKU.MP3]

七

shichi – **seven**

NOTE: BOTH "*SHICHI*" AND "*NANA*" ARE USED FOR 7. LEARN BOTH AND NOTE THE CONTEXT WHERE EACH IS USED. [SHICHI.MP3]

七

nana – **seven**

NOTE: BOTH "*SHICHI*" AND "*NANA*" ARE USED FOR 7. LEARN BOTH AND NOTE THE CONTEXT WHERE EACH IS USED. [NANA.MP3]

八

hachi – **eight**

[HACHI.MP3]

九

kyuu – **nine**

BOTH "KYUU" AND "KU" ARE USED FOR 9. LEARN BOTH AND NOTE THE CONTEXT WHERE EACH IS USED. [KYUU.MP3]

九

ku – **nine**

BOTH "*KYUU*" AND "*KU*" ARE USED FOR 9. LEARN BOTH AND NOTE THE CONTEXT WHERE EACH IS USED. [KU.MP3]

十

juu – **ten**

[JUU.MP3]

十一

juu ichi – **eleven**

10 AND 1 [JUUICHI.MP3]

十二

juu ni – **twelve**

10 AND 2 [JUUNI.MP3]

十三

juu san – **thirteen**

10 AND 3 [JUUSAN.MP3]

十四

juu yon – **fourteen**

THIS IS ALSO PRONOUNCED AS JUUSHI; 10 AND 4 [JUUYON.MP3]

十五

juu go – **fifteen**

10 AND 5 [JUUGO.MP3]

十六

juu roku – **sixteen**

10 AND 6 [JUUROKU.MP3]

十七

juu nana – seventeen

10 AND 7 [JUUNANA.MP3]

十八

juu hachi – eighteen

10 AND 8 [JUUHACHI.MP3]

十九

juu kyuu – nineteen

10 AND 9 [JUUKYUU.MP3]

二十

ni juu – twenty

2 AND 10 [NIJUU.MP3]

二十一

ni juu ichi – twenty one

2 AND 10 AND 1 [NIJUUICHI.MP3]

三十

san juu – **thirty**

3 AND 10 [SANJUU.MP3]

三十五

san juu go – **thirty five**

3 AND 10 AND 5 [SANJUUGO.MP3]

四十

yon juu – forty

4 AND 10 [YONJUU.MP3]

五十

go juu – **fifty**

5 AND 10 [GOJUU.MP3]

六十

roku juu – **sixty**

6 AND 10 [ROKUJUU.MP3]

七十

nana juu – **seventy**

7 AND 10 [NANAJUU.MP3]

八十

hachi juu – **eighty**

8 AND 10 [HACHIJUU.MP3]

九十

kyuu juu – **ninety**

9 AND 10 [KYUUJU.MP3]

百

hyaku – **one hundred**

[HYAKU.MP3]

千

sen – **one thousand**

[SEN.MP3]

一万

ichi man – ten thousand

LITERALLY "ONE TEN THOUSAND" [ICHIMAN.MP3]

二千八年

ni sen hachi nen – 2008 (year)

NOTE: YEARS ARE CONSTRUCTED BY THE NUMBER FOLLOWED BY "NEN"
[NISENHACHINEN.MP3]

Chapter Thirteen

Body Vocabulary

正座

seiza – **formal sitting**

LITTERALLY, "SITTING CORRECTLY." THIS IS SITTING STRAIGHT UP WITH LEGS FOLDED UNDER. [SEIZA.MP3]

腕

ude – **arm**

[UDE.MP3]

目

me – **eye**

[ME.MP3]

おなか

onaka – **stomach**

[ONAKA.MP3]

足

ashi – **leg/foot**

ASHI CAN BE EITHER "LEG" OR "FOOT." YOU CAN TELL BY THE CONTEXT. [ASHI.MP3]

足裏

ashi ura – **sole of foot**

ASHI (FOOT); *URA* (BACK) [ASHIURA.MP3]

足技

ashi waza – **foot techniques**

WAZA (TECHNIQUES) [ASHIWAZA.MP3]

中足

chuusoku – **ball of foot**

CHUU (MIDDLE) [CHUUSOKU.MP3]

胸

mune – **chest; breast**

[MUNE.MP3]

親指

oyayubi – **thumb**

LITERALLY, "PARENT FINGER." [OYAYUBI.MP3]

ひじ

hiji – **elbow**

[HIJI.MP3]

拳

kobushi – **fist**

[KOBUSHI.MP3]

指

yubi – **finger**

[YUBI.MP3]

足首

ashikubi – **ankle**

LITERALLY, "FOOT NECK." [ASHIKUBI.MP3]

おしり

oshiri – **buttocks**

[OSHIRI.MP3]

首

kubi – **neck**

[kubi.mp3]

手

te – **hand**

[TE.MP3]

手首

tekubi – **wrist**

LITTERALLY, "HAND NECK." [TEKUBI.MP3]

ひざ

hiza – **knee**

[HIZA.MP3]

頭

atama – **head**

[ATAMA.MP3]

鼻

hana – **nose**

[HANA.MP3]

背中

senaka – **back**

[SENAKA.MP3]

かた

kata – **shoulder**

[KATA.MP3]

かかと

kakato – **heel**

[KAKATO.MP3]

小手

kote – **forearm**

LITERALLY, "SMALL HAND." [KOTE.MP3]

体さばき

tai sabaki – **body movement**

TAI (BODY); *SABAKI* (HANDLING) [TAISABAKI.MP3]

下着

shitagi – **trousers / underwear**

LITERALLY, "UNDER CLOTHING." [SHITAGI.MP3]

上着

uwagi – **jacket**

LITERALLY, "OVER CLOTHING." [UWAGI.MP3]

Chapter Fourteen

Days of the Week

日曜日

nichiyōbi – **Sunday**

ALL DAYS OF THE WEEK END WITH "YŌBI." *NICHI* MEANS "SUN."
[NICHIYOUBI.MP3]

月 曜日

getsuyōbi – **Monday**

GETSU (MOON) [GETSUYOUBI.MP3]

火曜日

kayōbi – **Tuesday**

KA (FIRE) [KAYOUBI.MP3]

水曜日

suiyōbi – **Wednesday**

SUI (WATER) [SUIYOUBI.MP3]

木曜日

mokuyōbi – **Thursday**

MOKU (WOOD) [MOKUYOUBI.MP3]

金曜日

kinyōbi – **Friday**

KIN (GOLD) [KINYOUBI.MP3]

土曜日

doyōbi – **Saturday**

DO (GROUND; EARTH) [DOYOUBI.MP3]

Chapter Fifteen

Seasons

春

haru – **spring**

[HARU.MP3]

夏

natsu – **summer**

[NATSU.MP3]

秋

aki – **fall; autumn**

[AKI.MP3]

冬

fuyu – **winter**

[FUYU.MP3]

Chapter Sixteen

Months of the Year

一月

ichi gatsu – **January**

MONTHS IN JAPANESE ARE EASY; THEY ARE SIMPLY THE NUMBER AND "GATSU" (MONTH) [ICHIGATSU.MP3]

二月

ni gatsu – **February**

SECOND MONTH [NIGATSU.MP3]

三月

san gatsu – **March**

THIRD MONTH [SANGATSU.MP3]

四月

shi gatsu – **April**

IT ISN'T "*YONGATSU.*" FOURTH MONTH [SHIGATSU.MP3]

五月

go gatsu – **May**

FIFTH MONTH [GOGATSU.MP3]

六月

roku gatsu – **June**

SIXTH MONTH [ROKUGATSU.MP3]

七月

shichi gatsu – **July**

SEVENTH MONTH [SHICHIGATSU.MP3]

八月

hachi gatsu – **August**

EIGHTH MONTH [HACHIGATSU.MP3]

九月

ku gatsu – **September**

NINTH MONTH [KUGATSU.MP3]

十月

juu gatsu – **October**

TENTH MONTH [JUUGATSU.MP3]

十一月

juu ichi gatsu – **November**

ELEVENTH MONTH [JUUICHIGATSU.MP3]

十二月

juu ni gatsu – **December**

TWELTH MONTH [JUUNIGATSU.MP3]

Chapter Seventeen

Counting Days

Counting days in Japanese is a little harder than the months. You'll have to memorize most of these.

一日

tsuitachi – **first (of the month)**

[TSUITACHI.MP3]

一日

ichi nichi – **one day**

NOTICE THE KANJI ARE THE SAME, BUT THE PRONUNCIATION TELLS US IF IT IS THE NAME OF THE DAY OR JUST SAYING IT IS "ONE DAY." [ICHINICHI.MP3]

二日

futsuka – **2nd (of the month); 2 days**

[FUTSUKA.MP3]

三日

mikka – **3rd (of the month); 3 days**

[MIKKA.MP3]

四日

yokka – **4th (of the month); 4 days**

[YOKKA.MP3]

五日

itsuka − 5th (of the month); 5 days

[ITSUKA.MP3]

六日

muika − 6th (of the month); 6 days

[MUIKA.MP3]

七日

nanoka − 7th (of the month); 7 days

[NANOKA.MP3]

八日

yōka − 8th (of the month); 8 days

[YOUKA.MP3]

九日

kokonoka − 9th (of the month); 9 days

[KOKONOKA.MP3]

十日

tooka − 10th (of the month); 10 days

[TOOKA.MP3]

十一日

juu ichi nichi − 11th (of the month); 11 days

THE REST MOSTLY FOLLOW THE CHINESE READINGS FOR NUMBERS PLUS "NICHI". THE EXCEPTIONS ARE 14TH, 20TH AND 24TH. (SEE BELOW)
[JUUICHINICHI.MP3]

十四日

juu yokka − 14th (of the month); 14 days

THE 14TH IS AN EXCEPTION. [JUUYOKKA.MP3]

二十日

hatsuka − 20th (of the month); 20 days

THE 20TH IS AN EXCEPTION. [HATSUKA.MP3]

二十四日

ni juu yokka − 24th (of the month); 24 days

THE 24TH IS AN EXCEPTION. [NIJUUYOKKA.MP3]

二十八日

ni juu hachi nichi – **28th (of the month); 28 days**

ALL THE REST ARE REGULAR LIKE THIS ONE. [NIJUUHACHINICHI.MP3]

DOWNLOAD LINK

Download Link for the MP3s:

https://japanesereaders.com/1059-2/

Thank you for purchasing and reading this book! To contact the authors, please email them at help@thejapanshop.com. See also the wide selection of materials for learning Japanese at www.TheJapanShop.com and the free site for learning Japanese www.thejapanesepage.com.

Printed in Great Britain
by Amazon

53283637R00056